Supernatural Dartmoor

Michael Williams

Bossiney Books · Launceston

Acknowledgements

I am deeply grateful to the people, especially members of the Ghost Club Society, who have given me interviews and authors who have allowed me to quote from their works. Thanks also to my wife Sonia and to Elaine Beckton who have been allies on so many projects – and last but not least to Jane and Paul White for the chance to write once more for Bossiney.

First published 2003 by
Bossiney Books Ltd, Langore, Launceston, Cornwall PL15 8LD
www.bossineybooks.co.uk
ISBN 1-899383-55-7

Printed in Great Britain by R Booth (Troutbeck Press), Mabe, Cornwall

Some other Bossiney books which may be of interest

Dowsing in Devon and Cornwall by Alan Neal
Ghost hunting South-West by Michael Williams
Ghostly encounters South-West by Peter Underwood
Ghosts of Devon by Peter Underwood
Ghosts of North Devon by Peter Underwood
Psychic phenomena of the West by Michael Williams
Spiritual guides in the West Country by Jane E White
Supernatural in the West by Michael Williams
UFOs over Devon by Jonathan Downes
Weird Devon by Jonathan Downes

Introduction

Dartmoor is a world of its own: granite tors and sweeping moorland, wide skies and wooded valleys, cottages and farms and peat-coloured streams are among its many glorious visual qualities.

Hidden elements in the landscape hold more ghosts and paranormal activity than any other comparable part of Devon. This great wilderness is unique. You cannot go far on the moor without encountering genuine ghostly claims.

In the manor at Wonson, for instance, four Cavaliers have been seen playing cards. In other parts of Devon phantom black dogs have been encountered, but on Cator Common a ghostly white dog has been observed. And at Gidleigh, local people maintain they have heard the sounds of a bloody fight. There are dozens of such happenings around the moor.

Ghost hunting is often a curious business. For hours in an investigation nothing happens. Then suddenly something defying all logic occurs – and that makes the occasion.

The important thing for the ghost hunter is to explore dispassionately, ideally in the company of kindred spirits. An individual operating alone can be tricked by a change of light, a shadow, an excited imagination.

I believe in the reality of ghosts – seeing is believing. So much so, that after nearly forty years of psychical exploration I now veer to the view that limits exist only in our minds.

So, why is Dartmoor such a haunted area?

The question is inevitable, but the answer – or answers – remain elusive. A growing number of psychic investigators, including the eminent Colin Wilson, believe there is a powerful link between ghosts and stone – and Dartmoor is, of course, a stone-scattered landscape. Many of us feel that, in some curious way, stone can somehow 'absorb emanations'. Dartmoor also has a great number of rivers: from the northern heights rise as

many as six and from the southern slopes there are another four. Does this river presence have something to do with the fact that Dartmoor is such haunted territory? I have to say, yes, it seems that water does indeed trigger many manifestations – springs, underground streams, wells, rivers and the sea itself often provide the setting for paranormal activity.

In my experience, ghosts could also be tied to what we call time. It is tempting to suppose that when we see a ghost, we are somehow looking out from our own time frame and observing events in another.

Is atmospheric location perhaps another facet of the explanation? Though ghosts manifest themselves in modern buildings and on trains and planes, a high percentage appear in and around old buildings and ruins. And here on Dartmoor, especially in the remoter regions, there is a sense of stepping back into history. The obscure, very distant past is somehow reflected in that phase of twilight when the tors take on an even more sinister air – and the whole landscape is like something out of an Alfred Hitchcock film. (As an interesting aside, green and grey are the predominant colours in the landscape and, intriguingly, green is rated the colour which links Nature and the supernatural.)

In the field of modern crime investigation, the police pay increasing attention to photographic evidence. And in the paranormal field, the camera also has a key part to play: it often freezes a crucial moment and captures that which defies and defeats the cynic.

In simple terms, the process of taking a photograph – whether by a professional like Lord Lichfield, or by a holidaymaker simply snapping on the moor – requires certain elements: someone to hold the camera, a good film inside it, and a subject worth photographing. I believe something similar happens when we

Opposite: Water and stone are both conducive to ghostly manifestations – and Dartmoor is abundant in both, as here at Becky Falls

Great Hound Tor provokes powerful reactions in many visitors

are ghost hunting. The ghost is a kind of image which leaves a sort of imprint. Just as a camera needs someone knowledgeable to use it, ghosts are probably only visible to a certain type of person. And it does not end there. We need to be in the right place at the right time.

Great Hound Tor

The tors of Dartmoor are among the splendours of the whole Devon landscape, and out on the heights you wonder about the mystery of time, for a sense of age and timelessness cloaks the landscape. J B Priestley believed there are three types of time: 'ordinary time' when, for example, we stand on Plymouth Station waiting for a train; 'inner time' when we are quietly contemplating; and 'creative time' when a writer or painter enters a phase of intensity and creativity.

My favourite tor is Great Hound Tor, North-east of Widecombe and about 1½ km south of Manaton, it stands just 450 metres high, but you get the impression you are on a mountain top. The land rolls away from you like an ocean and you really experience a feeling of wilderness. When one of the television companies recreated Sir Arthur Conan Doyle's novel *The Hound of the Baskervilles*, some of the filming took place around Great Hound Tor. Sir Arthur, of course, knew the moor well. A real all-rounder, he was the creator of Sherlock Holmes and Dr Watson, a Spiritualist, a keen student of paranormal phenomena, and he was convinced telepathy worked between human beings. An early member of The Ghost Club Society, he also researched the possibility of messages being relayed from the dead.

Great Hound Tor has a powerful atmosphere, and different people respond in different ways – some find it unbearable; others, who have tried to overcome an inexplicable fear, have fallen into a trance, but nobody understands why.

I must confess I've never had any such reaction on my score-or-so visits, but on several occasions I have been aware of an unseen presence, and have had the distinct feeling that I was being watched. Sometimes I've sensed a presence immediately behind me, but on turning round sharply I felt I was a second too late to see who or what it was. My lovely collie dog, Rex, who accompanied me on several visits to haunted properties, invariably had an air of excited anticipation around this tor.

Interestingly, about three years ago, Rachael Smith-Rawnsley, one of our Ghost Club Society members who lives in London, came to the summit with her black labrador Ruby and the animal bounded around with great enthusiasm and, more significantly, unleashed a few rare growls. 'It was quite out of character,' said Rachael, 'especially as there was nothing threatening in the vicinity.' Did Ruby pick up something beyond human vision?

The reaction of animals can be very revealing – confirmation that something is not quite of this world?

Kitty Jay's grave

Below Hound Tor, beyond the crossroads, is Kitty Jay's grave, 'the tenderest of all moorland memorials'. During her short life, Kitty was only a servant girl, but she has since grown into a Dartmoor heroine. She was seduced by the squire's son in the big house nearby, thrown out of her work and, desolate and deserted, she committed suicide. Like so many suicides of her time, she could not be buried in consecrated ground, so she lies here at the junction of three parishes – Manaton, North Bovey and Widecombe.

In 1978 I saw a quite extraordinary television programme concerning Kitty Jay. Joe Keeton, a hypnotist living and working in the Wirral, came to the old Westward studios at Derry's Cross, Plymouth. He had been regressing (taking back to an earlier life) a nurse called Pauline McKay who also lived in the Wirral.

Pauline had never been to the South-west but, under hypnosis, she 'became Kitty Jay, a Devonshire servant girl' who had committed suicide near Chagford in the late 1700s.

Mr Keeton wrote to the Westcountry Studies Library at Exeter asking if they knew of a Kitty Jay. He was surprised to receive a reply saying Jay's grave was on the edge of Dartmoor and that the servant girl had hanged herself at Canna Farm.

During the TV programme Pauline, under hypnosis, gave the impression that she 'knew' the Dartmoor area, describing where she and the squire's son went for walks. She told how he later deserted her and talked of her own suicide.

Barney Camfield, who conducted services at a Unitarian church on Dartmoor and who took part in the programme, told me he was convinced Pauline McKay was genuine.

Anyway, no matter what time of year you come to Kitty Jay's roadside grave (it lies just in the path to the wood, shaded by tall trees), there are always fresh flowers on it. Although there have been sightings of a strange dark figure hovering around the grave, mysteriously, no one knows who puts these flowers here.

In October 2001, when a group of Ghost Club Society members came to the grave, our mediums were convinced they made contact with Kitty's spirit. Moreover they uncovered the fact that the tradition of flowers on the grave was started by Beatrice Chase of Widecombe. Beatrice was a great Dartmoor character, a woman who became a legend in her eccentric lifetime. Her real name was Olive Katherine Parr. A Roman Catholic, she claimed to be a direct descendant of Catherine Parr, the sixth wife of Henry VIII. Hers is a curious story and her love affair with Dartmoor lasted more than half a century.

She came with her invalid mother to the moor around the beginning of the 20th century and started writing romantic books, full of the praise of God and Dartmoor's varied beauties. Another writer, John Oxenham, used her name for the heroine in one of his novels whose title, *My Lady of the Moor*, Beatrice graciously adopted. Moreover she lived up to the grand title to such an extent that she would accost strangers and present them with a sprig of white heather, 'giving' them the 'freedom' of the moor!

Her books caught the nuances of Dartmoor in the old days and are worth tracking down in second-hand bookshops. She is buried in the lovely green-grey churchyard at Widecombe, 'The Cathedral of the Moor'.

As to who carries on the tradition of placing flowers on Kitty's grave, it remains a mystery.

The Three Crowns at Chagford

In October 2000 I was leading a team of Ghost Club Society members on a tour of some haunted locations on Dartmoor and chose The Three Crowns at Chagford for a lunchtime stop.

Apart from it being a lovely building (Charles Kingsley called it 'a beautiful old mullioned and gabled perpendicular inn'), it has an excellent reputation for bar meals and, over the years, for the strange occurrences that have happened here.

A portrait of the young Cornishman Sydney Goldophin, Cavalier and poet who died after a set-to with Cromwell's Roundheads, hangs in the Goldophin lounge. Aged only 32 and already MP for Helston in Cornwall, Sydney was among Cavalier forces who set out to surprise the Parliamentarians billeted in Chagford. But they failed, and he was hit just above the knee by a musket ball. He fell from his horse, was taken to the porch of the inn, and died from his wounds.

John Poole, the duty manager at The Three Crowns, told us Sydney Godolphin's ghost has been seen and heard pacing the corridors on many occasions. Apparently he is inclined to be upset when alterations are made to the hotel. He is also a rather conceited ghost: one day a photographer had great problems taking a shot of the Godolphin lounge but when he included Sydney's portrait, all went well.

The Three Crowns at Chagford, haunted by the young Cavalier Sydney Godolphin, who died in the porch

The Three Crowns was built as a manor house by John Whiddon (sometimes spelt Whyddon), who went to London in the reign of King Henry VIII, became a lawyer and was knighted. During our visit, there was a curious coincidence: two members of this historic Whiddon family of Chagford, who had just booked into the hotel, joined us for a talk by John Poole. They were Americans on holiday and obviously knew nothing of our plans. They told me John's talk and our presence were a wonderful unexpected bonus.

Two of our members had an even stranger experience. They became aware of a door moving – and there was simply no rational explanation for the movement. As one of them commented, 'It were as if an unseen someone was flapping the door.'

After lunch Michael Wreford, Dartmoor raconteur, historian and Chagford cricketer, talked to us in the parish church, opposite the inn, about strange happenings in the area. And during

his talk I heard distinct footsteps pacing the aisle – but I took no great notice of them, assuming another person not involved with our group was looking around or attending to some church business.

Later, however, several members of our group said that when they heard the footsteps they turned around and the aisle was completely empty, though the footsteps continued. A spirit confirming Chagford's haunted reputation?

Supernatural sounds seem to be on the increase and there is an interesting theory that some noises can be 'recorded' in some minerals, notably stone. Under certain conditions or circumstances, these sounds can be played back – rather like a cassette playing back music. Granite is thought to be one of the most suitable rocks for this curious process.

My files contain accounts of people hearing all sorts of things, from a woman's high-heeled shoes and horses' hoofbeats to the snoring of a pig (which turned out to be a real pig fast asleep!) and music.

Often there is nothing vague about such reports either. A family from Cornwall were picnicking on the slopes of Brentor one day, listening to some beautiful music coming from within the tiny church. After their picnic they decided to go inside – and found it empty!

Mavis at Easton Court Hotel

Easton Court Hotel, just below the village of Chagford, is a delightful thatched house with granite walls and oak beams. It was built for a knight of the realm around 1450 and, for the last eight decades, has been run as a hotel. The present owners Debra and Paul Witting gave up high-flying jobs in the City to take on the considerable refurbishment needed and opened their doors to guests in 2001.

Opposite: Chagford Church, directly in front of the Three Crowns

Easton Court is one of those places where you feel a strong aura of the past. Evelyn Waugh spent three months here writing *Brideshead Revisited.* The Poet Laureate Sir John Betjeman stayed here, too, as did another scribe, John Steinbeck, not to mention assorted royals from former times.

The hotel also boasts a friendly ghost. Paul Witting told me: 'She walks around the oldest part of the building, making sure all is well. She is very benevolent to Debra and myself, and, according to a medium lady who stayed with us, she likes the two of us and what we are doing. She was called Mavis and died approximately two hundred years ago at the age of 45-50. She was a governess or senior housekeeper.

'Recent sightings have been made by me (twice) and one of our guests in 2001. The most recent sighting was by me a few weeks ago. She wears a grey uniform with white collar and cuffs, dark buttons down the front of her dress, and has her hair tied back in a loose bun. She looks efficient, not severe, and walks very purposefully.

'Our housekeeper has been with the hotel for the past twenty-three years and has never seen the ghost, but does find that things move around the bedrooms, such as mirrors being taken off hooks and placed against a wall on the opposite side of the room. And more recently, a tub of talcum powder was moved from the bathroom shelf and placed on the floor across the room – with no spillage! All in all, we are happy that she is here, and I personally am thrilled whenever I see her.'

Some Dartmoor coincidences

Do coincidences come under the supernatural umbrella?

I am inclined to think so. Arthur Koestler, who researched the subject, coined the phrase 'puns of destiny' to describe the phenomenon. I have certainly had some curious 'puns of destiny' relating to Dartmoor.

Easton Court Hotel

As a young journalist in West Cornwall I interviewed a painter and writer called Charles Simpson. It was one of those rare occasions when an interview turned into genuine friendship. Charles Simpson became not only a friend but a profound influence, encouraging me to absorb the landscape and let it speak.

Some years after his death, I came to the Scorhill Stone Circle on Dartmoor with my psychic friend Shirley Wallis and the photographer Ray Bishop. It was my first visit to the circle, but at the time I said, 'I feel so at home here I feel I must have been here before.'

'Perhaps someone close to you in the past has been here,' reflected Shirley, 'and you're picking up their vibes.'

Months later I was talking to Charles Simpson's daughter, Leonora, and she asked about my visit to Dartmoor. I mentioned the Scorhill Circle and Leonora responded by giving a surprising piece of information: 'My parents lived for some years at Tavistock and being so close to Dartmoor that was how my father first became interested in stone circles. I'm sure he drew and painted the Scorhill Circle.'

There was though – for me – another odd twist. Later still, a relation sent me some photographs of my late grandfather, Edgar Williams, who was a considerable influence in my formative years, and there among the photographs was one of him at the Scorhill Circle!

But perhaps an even odder Dartmoor coincidence took place in 1995 when I was rewriting the opening chapter of a book on the paranormal. On the Monday afternoon I was about halfway through the chapter and I began thinking about John William Dunne's book *An Experiment with Time*. It was first published as long ago as March 1927 and I was becoming aware of the fact that I needed a copy for my library. Mr Dunne was no crackpot; he was an old school army officer 'crossed with a mathematician and an aeronautical engineer'. He was not a time-haunted man either, like J B Priestley, but he was driven to try to prove a personal theory about time and he was strangely compelled to make some sense of the precognitive quality of his dream life.

Anyway that night I dreamt about time and a clock. Next morning I was committed to two calls on Dartmoor on business, and, driving across the moor, I suddenly decided to call in at the Dartmoor Bookshop at Ashburton, on the off-chance. I asked Barbara, the proprietress, if she had Dunne's *An Experiment with Time* and she immediately produced a 1934 edition. I certainly had had no intention of searching for a copy when I started the piece of writing the previous afternoon.

So what do we make of that? It wasn't the sort of book that would be on every bookseller's shelves!

Dartmoor has this knack of springing surprises. Take, for example, the case of Mr Harry Baskerville, the driver of a horse-drawn vehicle which took Sir Arthur Conan Doyle on his jour-

A hut circle at Grimspound

neys across Dartmoor. Little did Harry realise that as a result of these excursions his name, one day, would be immortalised in *The Hound of the Baskervilles.*

It was at Grimspound that Sir Arthur laid his plot for Sherlock Holmes to solve. James Turner called the place 'one of the most open and haunted parts of the moor'. I have never seen a ghost here. But, in the eye of the imagination, you can visualise the Bronze Age people with their sheep and cattle and their huts of granite blocks. Such locations give Dartmoor a timeless quality. Certainly when I first came to Grimspound I immediately thought of Dr Johnson's words: 'All that is really known on the ancient state of Britain is contained in a few pages...'

James died suddenly in 1975 – I was asked to identify his body – and I suppose it is a 'pun of destiny' that I should be seated at his old desk, writing these words about Dartmoor and the paranormal. It's the same desk where he wrote many books, including one about ghosts in the South-west in which he described a visit to Sabine-Baring Gould's haunted rectory at Lew Trenchard on the edge of the moor.

Hairy Hands at Postbridge

Is it possible for a psychic phenomenon to take control of a motor car?

Some people feel that the Hairy Hands of Postbridge are simply part of Dartmoor's folklore. Others have had horrific experiences when driving along the Postbridge road.

Rufus Endle was a thoroughly professional journalist who always insisted on the facts. One day we were enjoying a drink at his club near Plymouth Hoe, when he discovered I was researching a book on the paranormal. Rufus told me how, one night, driving back from Chagford where he had been working on a newspaper story, he had had a terrifying experience at Postbridge, on the road that leads to Princetown.

'Until that night, I had always regarded the Hairy Hands as pure legend – a good yarn for visitors. I'd had a couple of drinks during the interview back in Chagford… these were in the pre-breathaliser days… but I was quite sober. Suddenly, as I approached the bridge, a pair of hands gripped the driving wheel and I had to fight for control. It was a very scary minute or so. God knows how I didn't crash at the bridge, and the hands went as inexplicably as they came. I never wrote about it in the newspapers, or even told anybody else for fear of ridicule. You're the first person I've told, but don't use it until I'm dead and gone…'

Back in 1980, when Sally Jones was collecting material for a West Country book, she unearthed a matching account. This was from a Somerset doctor who, in 1977, informed her that at Postbridge, although he did not see any manifestation, he was aware of some powerful force inside his car: 'something quite out of my control…' In his case 'the steering wheel seemed to go wild'.

Around the same time I heard of a very serious driving accident on the same stretch of road, and a hardened media man said to me quietly: 'I reckon it's those bloody Hairy Hands

Simply a dangerous corner? Or the haunt of a homicidal spirit with a dislike of cars and motor cycles?

again…' But, like Rufus Endle, he asked me not to quote him.

There is no doubt some people are reluctant to 'go public' on supernatural subjects.

When I was writing my very first book on the supernatural, in the early 1970s, I was told that the distinguished actress Ann Todd had had certain paranormal experiences. I wrote to her and she replied in a very friendly spirit, writing in her own hand; I still have her letter, penned in red ink, in my files. Miss Todd explained at some length why 'I cannot lend my name to your book. I once, some years ago, gave some personal impressions of certain paranormal activity that I had had, and before I knew where I was the press was on me, misquoting and generally being very unhelpful.'

Other people feel more able to speak out. Hugh Pratt, writing to me from Lifton in June 2002, had this to say: 'I have heard several stories of a furry paw taking control of cars and causing otherwise unexplained accidents near Postbridge. Most of these accidents seem to have occurred between the Cherry Brook bridge and the Archerton turning... a nice straight bit of road! I think it may also have been active on the other side of the Dart. I have not heard of any trouble since before the Second World War. I have an open mind on the subject.'

Like Hugh, I am persuaded by the evidence that some strange things have really happened to motorists on the road around Postbridge. I also heard recently of a curious cycling experience on this same road. Maurice Dart was then living at St Budeaux, Plymouth, and this is what he told me:

'In June 1955 I had travelled to North Bovey to attend the Fair, going up by train to Moretonhampstead and then cycling on the Saturday. I was cycling home across Dartmoor on the lovely warm sunny Sunday morning, really enjoying the experience and stopping at places to take in the gorgeous scenery.

'Having passed through Postbridge and heading for Princetown, I entered a section of road bounded by trees and thickets. For some reason panic gripped me, and I looked back and upwards over my left shoulder and saw what appeared to be a swirling cloudy mass in the otherwise clear blue sky descending rapidly towards me.

'Having sensed something there, the panic grew and I lost all sense of reason. I changed down a gear and pedalled as hard and fast as I was able to until I had come out of the wooded section, passed through Two Bridges and was ploughing up the hill. At this point, all of a sudden the feeling of panic left me just as suddenly as it had arrived, and I turned and looked over my shoulder again and just glimpsed the fuzzy mass disappearing up into the sky, way behind me. I continued on my way very bemused and puzzled. At this time I knew nothing about the Hairy Hands, not becoming aware of their existence until I purchased a copy of *The Folklore and Witchcraft of Dartmoor* by Ruth St Leger-Gordon (published in 1965), in which I read about them.

I immediately thought back to my experience ten years previously.'

Mr Pratt also passed on the eerie experience of an old retired farm worker in the 1920s: 'He had walked up through Twist Lane, which leads from Smeardon Down, above Peter Tavy, through to the open moor, when he saw a crow with a broken wing flapping about in front of him. He wanted to finish it off and struck out with his shovel. The crow dodged out of the way. He struck again and again, but the crow always evaded him.

'As it led him on he heard it saying in a crow-like voice, "Walkety, Walkety!" Eventually it led him to Stephen's grave where it disappeared into the ground.

'Stephen's grave is marked by a small standing stone with an "S" inscribed on its base [Grid Ref: SX536781]. Stephen was a young man who lived at Rodge Farm, probably about 1650. He killed himself when crossed in love and, as a suicide, was buried on the moor at the intersection of two tracks. This custom is centuries older than Christianity, but it's amazing how recently it was practised!'

Brentor – and ley lines

You cannot travel far across Dartmoor and not be aware of the towering presence of Brentor. All the tors add majesty and magic to the green-grey landscape, but there are few more beautiful, more impressive landmarks in the whole of the West Country than Brentor.

Dedicated to St Michael, the 14th-century church on its summit is the fourth smallest in England, just 11.3 metres long and 4.4 metres wide. Standing more than 300 metres above sea level, there is no road for a car.

Brentor is on a famous 'ley line' which begins at Carn Les Boel at Land's End, West Cornwall, and goes on to Glastonbury in Somerset, Avebury in Wiltshire, and beyond. Leys came to

Brentor Church, at an altitude of more than 300 metres and with no road access. Only the fit visit or worship here, and even brides have to walk up the steep slope

prominence more than seventy years ago when a man called Alfred Watkins noted from maps and careful research that pre-historic remains and ancient churches fell into alignments. He called these alignments 'leys'. Mr Watkins was no occultist, and when he made his thoughts public he was in his mid sixties, a businessman and a magistrate.

In his younger days Alfred was a representative for his father's firm, and he rode many miles across the Herefordshire country-side. A lover of the landscape, he had a special interest in ancient sites. On the afternoon of 20 June 1921, riding his horse across the hills near Brewardine, a shaft of inspiration suddenly hit him: he realised that the British landscapes are criss-crossed by old paths and tracks. And from that afternoon his interest in the subject of leys expanded and deepened.

Other people became intrigued too, and country lovers everywhere started searching for ley lines and reporting back to Mr Watkins at the Straight Track Postal Club. Their rules were strict: a ley line had to be acknowledged by at least several independent observers or witnesses.

A reference to leys would be incomplete without a brief mention of earth energies. Our knowledge of these probably stems from China, where the art of divining earth energies as they flow along the leys – or 'dragon paths' as the Chinese call them – enabled people to decide where best to build a house or temple. They looked for an area that would harmonise with the flow of energy from the earth. So when we come to Brentor and feel it is 'a good place', we are no doubt part of a long tradition of people sensing the positive vibrations of Nature. At one time men's and women's instincts were so finely tuned that on occasion they must have felt they were almost part of the sky and the rugged landscape around them.

Even today, whenever I go to Brentor I invariably have a powerful sense of well being. I asked Plymouth author and broadcaster Shirley Wallis about this. Shirley, who lectures on the paranormal and is a psychic researcher, said quite simply: 'Brentor is a great place for all reasons, all levels of experience. If you have a problem, take it there and you will return with a sense of balance and solution.'

Rachael Smith-Rawnsley's dog Ruby had a curious experience on the top of Brentor in October 2001. Rachael had been thinking of a well-known Royal Naval personality with royal connections, someone with a genuine interest in the paranormal. But his name eluded her.

Then, suddenly on the summit the dog, seemingly reading her mind, led her to a grave. As Rachael put it: 'For some unknown reason I was trying to recall this man's name on the way across Dartmoor. Just outside Brentor Church Ruby dragged me off to the headstone of a person whose name immediately triggered the one I'd been wanting to remember. It was more than a coincidence.'

I have seen Ruby on an earlier Ghost Club Society tour apparently pinpoint the precise spot of a murder, all of which reinforces the view of the celebrated Irish ghost hunter Elliot O'Donnell who once said: 'When I investigate a haunted house I generally take a dog with me, because experience has taught me that a dog seldom fails to give notice in some way or another.'

The nature of ghosts

You do not have to travel far on Dartmoor before realising odd powers are at work, and if you seriously investigate or hunt the phantoms of this great wilderness a crucial question will naturally come to mind.

What is a ghost?

There are characters who keep coming back in ghostly form. There are historical ghosts which usually appear in or around old properties or ancient landscapes. But what about modern ghosts, even ghosts of the living? Animal ghosts too and haunted objects like Drake's drum?

Unfortunately, we have to face the fact that there is a huge variety of manifestation – so much so there is probably more than one explanation.

The other big problem is we have not yet found out the precise circumstances which unleash ghosts, although there has to be a common denominator. When we make that discovery, we shall have made an enormous leap forward – to such a degree that we may be able to produce a ghost at will.

I believe we may not get the full answer until we discover what happens after the thing we call death. I further believe that a ghost will, one day, almost certainly give us some of the answers.

There have been rare cases of conversations between the living and the dead. If such conversations can be caught on film and tape, then doors of understanding will open. In the meantime it is important that we continue to investigate with fair and open minds, our feet firmly planted on the ground in the here and now.

Lydford Castle

Lydford Castle is a place to send shivers down our spines.

This grey cube of stone once struck terror into the hearts and minds of the innocent and the guilty. Times were when it was the tinners' gaol – and it had a wicked reputation.

In the 1600s the Tavistock poet William Browne came here, visiting his friend Colonel James Hals, a prisoner of war and a Parliamentarian. Lydford Castle was then under the command of Sir Richard Grenville, King Charles's General in the West.

The poet was appalled and moved to write:

> I oft have heard of Lydford law
> How in the morn they hang and draw
> And sit in judgement after.
> At first I wondered at it much,
> But since I've found the matter such
> That it deserves no laughter.

Better, he penned, 'to be stoned, pressed or hanged than pass a night in that dread pit.'

That elegant writer and gentleman, the late James Mildren, had this to say about Lydford Castle:

'The old ground floor was filled in with rubble except, significantly, for a small pit. That was to be a place of chilling horror, an abominable black hole. It could be reached only by ladder –

Lydford Castle

an unlit and dreaded chamber of the damned. The rubble has now been cleared away yet, to this very day, workmen sent down there on ropes to clear away the litter and debris still experience, though only momentarily, the horror of this hell-hole.'

So much for its grisly history, what of its paranormal reputation? About ten years ago, David Farrant, President of the British Psychic and Occult Society, told me of an all-night vigil at Lydford Castle. A trained alsation dog 'froze' at the top of a wrought-iron staircase leading to the dungeons and repeatedly barked at an invisible something below; and when carried down the stairs the animal cringed in a corner. Later, at precisely ten minutes to three, a dark shape, resembling a bear, materialised in an adjacent area and seemed to glide along before disappearing below a stone archway, leaving behind it an icy cold atmosphere. Someone attempted to photograph this fleeting apparition, but the negatives, when later developed, were blank.

Julia Quinn is a medium with a fast rising reputation. She came to Lydford Castle for the first time in 2001. I asked her for her impressions.

'First of all,' she said, 'my pendulum went haywire. So many things there… mixed things. There's a lot of atmosphere about the place. Almost too much atmosphere to pinpoint one thing. At night I'd think it would be a very frightening spot. Even in daylight I felt uneasy in parts… something quite unpleasant. The past is almost the present… that's the impression.'

Okehampton Castle

James Turner, who wrote so evocatively about the landscape, encouraged me to acquire a taste for ruins. In 1947, James bought 'the most haunted house in England', Borley Rectory – or what was left of it. He had an interesting theory that some ghosts are so lifelike many people go through life never realising they have seen one – or several!

Anyway, I took his advice about ruins, and my first Devonshire discovery was Okehampton Castle. An important gateway to the moor, the town of Okehampton has a supernatural reputation and I soon discovered these castle ruins are haunted by the ghost of a beautiful but complex lady who lived in the first half of the 17th century. They call her 'the wicked Lady Howard'. Some say she murdered husbands and killed two of her children. There were whispers, among the gossips, that she was 'an unnatural mother'.

But others say that Mary Howard's own ill treatment at the hands of her father, who was a sadist, deprived her of her maternal qualities. Whatever the case, many people are convinced she still wanders among these ruins.

In the 1980s I interviewed Clement Horn, who had been custodian of the castle for nearly ten years. Despite Mary's murderous reputation in life, Clement rated her 'a friendly spirit'. He told me: 'I saw Lady Howard on several occasions'.

Okehampton Castle

His most vivid sighting was late one afternoon: 'Just before I got to the chapel I saw this vision… I say vision because it was as if she belonged to another world. I stood still and watched her. When I was a boy I remember Baring-Gould telling me, "If you ever encounter a ghost, don't move and don't say anything!" Baring-Gould believed in ghosts!

'The interesting thing was that on this occasion I could see her very vividly; so much so that I could make out a slow movement, very slow. She was combing her hair, long black hair, over a white gown or cloak. I must have stood there two or three minutes watching her. Then suddenly she got up and walked away with her arms stretched out… she walked in the direction of the keep and disappeared.'

Ghost Club Society members came to these ruins in 2001 and our mediums were quite sure they made contact with Lady

Mary Howard. It was curious: when they asked for a sign of her presence, the trees in the vicinity stirred whereas the trees elsewhere hardly moved. A coincidence? Or something deeper?

I later asked Trevor Kenward, Ghost Club Society Council member and one of the most experienced ghost hunters in Britain, for his response to the place. Here is what he had to say:

'This weird and in some ways menacing ruin rises steeply from the river plain upon which the present town of Okehampton is now built. It cumulates in an earth bailey upon which are the remains of an oppressive keep, with the top of the east-facing wall defying all rules of gravity by staying in place.

'As I walked through the outer gatehouse I knew this location had many secrets hidden within its crumbling walls. Past the inner gatehouse I walked, uphill all the time – on my right were the remains of the Great Hall, pantry and kitchens. A steep climb did take me to the keep, a structure that dominates this location.

'It was on my downward walk, keeping to the south side of the buildings, that I entered the remains of the chapel and at once sensed a paranormal presence. It was female, perhaps in her late twenties, dressed in a long robe trimmed with white lace work around the top of the bodice, and perhaps a six-inch dark blue lace like trimming to the base of the skirt.

'But this was not a dress that would have been worn in a convent. She had gold chains around her neck and she had a very thick gold armlet. This would be, I am sure, a lady of some importance. May it have been Lady Howard I encountered in that long disused chapel? Stone walls, falling slowly as they weather with wind, rain and frost do their worst to cover the past…

'Okehampton Castle still keeps its secrets and its ghost walks these cold stone chambers, tantalising all who visit this very emotive location.'

The Widecombe storm

In this book I endeavour to stick to supernatural facts. However, no analysis of supernatural Dartmoor would be complete without some reference to the great Widecombe storm of 1639, a truly horrific event which undoubtedly took place but which has since become part of the fabric and folklore of the area.

These are the facts. On Sunday 21 October 1639, three hundred people came to the church at Widecombe for the evening service. A violent thunder storm erupted, and inside the beautiful church, dedicated to St Pancras, there was almost total darkness.

Suddenly a fiery ball shot through a window by the tower, tearing away a section of the roof and parts of the walls. The ball then plunged into the terrified congregation. Clothes were set alight and bodies singed. Richard Hill, who taught at Widecombe School at the time, described these happenings in verse – you can read them today on the boards in the church.

Mr Hill reckoned it was all 'an act of God' but many superstitious moorlanders pointed to the Devil himself.

It's here where the boundary between fact and folklore becomes well and truly blurred. The tradition is that the innkeeper at Poundsgate received a visit that very afternoon from a stranger on a black horse, a man who asked for directions to Widecombe Church. The tale gets better in that the stranger is said to have asked for a drink, and when the ale went down his throat there was a sizzling noise. Then the man carelessly allowed the innkeeper to see his cloven hoof – the Devil in person!

Happily none of that negativity lingers today. Widecombe Church has a great spirituality, and is a place 'to quieten the mind and compose the spirit'.

Nevertheless it is interesting to reflect that some ghosts only manifest during stormy weather. I know of one case of ghostly sounds – a horse-drawn carriage – only heard in rough weather. An indication perhaps that it came to grief in difficult conditions.

A medium's reaction to supernatural Dartmoor

Pamela Smith-Rawnsey is a medium of talent and integrity, her contributions to Ghost Club Society investigations often providing depth and insight. Using her crystal pendulum and powers of intuition, she is capable of uncovering a great deal of information about the past – and past lives.

I have travelled with her across Dartmoor on three occasions and have therefore asked for her reaction to the supernatural character of the moor.

Dartmoor, she believes, has different faces, different moods: 'When I was young it was a place of foreboding, evil doings and sudden terrible mists that enveloped the innocent and hid the guilty. But during visits in recent years I have discovered a different Dartmoor.

'It's a place of extraordinary beauty and tranquillity, full of mystery and sometimes great sadness. I've learnt to use a crystal pendulum and, thanks to your encouragement and others in the Society, I've become – to my own surprise – quite skilled in using it to make contact with the lost souls we sometimes encounter on our forays into the unknown.

'One such "lost soul" is Kitty Jay, whose grave at those crossroads near Hound Tor is a melancholy reminder of the harsh treatment meted out to young girls who were abused and then reviled in days gone by. Yet Kitty commands our attention still and there is a very powerful presence.

'As we gathered around her grave, attempting to make contact with her, a young man drew up on his motorbike. He looked distressed and I immediately felt we should move away until he had paid his respects. He stood for some moments at the head

A stone circle known as the Nine Stones at Belstone. Old untouched places such as this perhaps bring us closer to an understanding of time and of the paranormal

of the grave, head bowed, obviously in some private communion. One of our members spoke to him afterwards and he admitted he had made this journey every year on the same day. Such is the power of Kitty Jay.

'Dartmoor almost more than anywhere I've ever been abounds with strangeness. There are unexplained misty patches on the photographs we've taken around Kitty Jay's grave, and my pendulum goes like a Catherine wheel on the ancient stone bridge down by the stream, below the main bridge on the road above. Two of our members took a photograph, which shows a lone figure at the far end of the bridge. There was no one there when the photo was taken.

'We had many encounters with the paranormal on our two weekends on Dartmoor. I'm beginning to realise that if you wait long enough, everything comes to you here. I feel the door is opening on all aspects of the paranormal. I'm beginning to understand more about this ability I seem to have, but which I firmly believe everyone has, and I feel it's the old untouched places like Dartmoor which hold the key to our knowledge.

'The new technology we use in our search for answers is giving us clues and this, combined with the ancient knowledge within all of us, will unlock many doors. Because Dartmoor is one of the few untamed areas in Britain, it here is where we should be looking to tune into powerful Nature and uncover her secrets.

'The last time I stood on Dartmoor, in the midst of an ancient settlement, I felt sure we were drawing closer to an understanding of the paranormal, that time was in some way connected with our misunderstanding of death and that we are, in the twenty-first century, on the brink of an exciting, rewarding breakthrough...'

Ghost horses

As a horseman I have long been intrigued by the number of phantom horses we have here in the region. Responsible witnesses have seen them or heard ghostly hoofbeats. At Throwleigh, for example, witnesses say they felt a rush of a psychic wind as invisible equines galloped by.

Quite one of the oddest time slips occurred some years ago when two women riding in the vicinity of Hunter's Tor (above Lustleigh Cleave) came across a dozen men on horseback... there were others on foot and there were also some greyhounds... quite a little troupe. The odd thing is all the men were dressed in medieval costume. Must be actors on location for a film, they thought.

Very curious about this contingent, the two women followed them until the group of strange riders, horses, walkers and greyhounds were hidden by a stone wall. When the two modern women riders rode past the wall the medieval band had disappeared into thin air, and when they searched, neither woman could find any hoofprints in the soft ground… only those of their own horses.

Does the appearance of animal phantoms mean that animals go on beyond what we call death? I put this question to a very down-to-earth Irish veterinary surgeon who had a country practice here in the South-west and, after a lifelong involvement with animals, was sure. He stated rather emphatically, 'Some animals do go on…' Certainly on the basis of scientific tests, especially in the United States, the impression is that some animals are as 'human' as we think we are.

Horses, for their part, are very psychic. I heard of a case where many horses refused to enter a haunted wood and of other horses, once in the wood, behaving oddly and out of character.

Not long ago I was talking with an experienced horsewoman and she told me how horses pick up things in the atmosphere. There had been a bad road accident a few kilometres from her stables, and for a long time afterwards her horses reacted strangely whenever they came to the accident spot.

The Highwayman at Sourton

The Highwayman at Sourton is an exceptional hostelry and is a very apt gateway to the moor. It is full of curios and antiques, and oozes a strange, fascinating aura. Everywhere there is a strong whiff of the past: it's the kind of location that would have drawn Arthur Negus and Professor Joad like magnets, and ghost hunter Harry Price too – for there is a paranormal reputation here.

The inn is believed to have been an alehouse back in the 1280s. Then in 1620 it became The Golden Fleece. But when 'Buster' and Rita Jones took over the business in 1961 it was the New Inn.

The back of the Highwayman at Sourton, an unusual pub where unusual things happen

The front door opens into the upholstered coach which once ran from Okehampton to Launceston, and you step through another door into the central passage. On the right is the Hideaway Bar, where you can still see the original bar area but now you can even sit inside what was once the fireplace. On the left is the Coach Cabin, decorated with items relating to the old days of coaches and horses – and the phantom of a Cavalier is sometimes seen here.

And presiding over The Highwayman today is Sally Thomson, an Aries subject with green-blue eyes, daughter of Rita and Buster Jones. It attracts so many overseas visitors that Sally, who has a degree in languages, has had the history of the inn translated into Spanish and French.

There is a curious ambience about the whole establishment: in places you feel you are aboard ship and in others you get the impression you are in a religious building: there are many ecclesiastical aspects with Gothic arches which came from an old Plymouth church, and some of the panelling is from Sir Francis Drake's grand residence on the far side of the moor at Buckland Abbey. The Highwayman is a location that might have come straight out of a Gothic novel by the late Dame Iris Murdoch.

When you step into the Galleon Bar you somehow feel you've entered some magical time machine and have gone back in history. There is an impressive wooden door from an old sailing ship, a whaler called *Diana*, and the face on the door uncannily resembles a later tragic Diana. Curiously too there is a Prince of Wales emblem.

Here you really sense 'the puns of destiny' are at work and it is in this room that the Ghost Research Foundation International has held two seances. Sally Thomson attended both and was impressed by the integrity of all concerned: 'They made contact with an old sailor who was "stuck", and were able to release him and send him on his way. Interestingly many orbs were filmed and recorded and they seemed "to be coming out" of this ancient wooden door.'

Sally and the medium are certain the *Diana* sank and that lives were lost. They wonder whether these orbs might have been their spirits trapped within the very wood of the door.

'The Highwayman,' says Sally 'opens up people's imaginations but there is no doubt ghosts have been seen here, notably a Cavalier… my mother has seen him on many occasions; other people, too. There is a lady in a mop cap… she's been sighted as well. Personally I've not seen anything yet.'

During the last two years or so a number of bizarre things have happened at The Highwayman. Footsteps have been heard; Bruce, Sally's husband, saw a man enter the inn and then vanish; a psychic, paying her first visit, was convinced she saw various phantoms, including Sally's grandmother who spent many hours here in her lifetime; and an apparent vortex of energy has been captured on camera.

You don't need to be a clairvoyant to predict that one of these days (or more probably one of these nights) Sally will experience a happening that unquestionably defies all human logic. Truth is, something deep and secret lingers in this Aladdin's Cave. So much so, I believe major manifestations are likely to occur here. For all the atmosphere of the past, the future of The Highwayman is rich in paranormal possibility.

Other inns

The number of manifestations in and around inns prompts the question 'Why?' The Doubting Thomas will say, 'Such claims are aimed at generating more interest and more business in that particular inn or hotel...' There may be a grain of truth in some instances but, basically, in my considered opinion it is a fairly cynical comment.

Many of our Dartmoor inns are old, and for generations of families have been the hub of laughter and enjoyment. It could be that some people who have died are reluctant to leave such convivial surroundings – it is a paranormal fact that many ghostly characters are inclined to stick to a particular building or a clearly defined area.

But equally some ghosts do fade from the scene altogether. For example when I was planning the Ghost Club Society's tour of Dartmoor for October 2001, I talked to a member of the staff at the Old Inn, Widecombe, and he told me they had had no manifestations there for something like ten years.

I once raised this point with my old trusted friend Alan Nance, a Spiritualist with a great gift for healing. Alan believed 'After a period of time, sometimes lasting years, a spirit will accept the fact he or she is on the other side... and therefore happily settles there and has no wish to return to their earlier earthly places.'

But there are, of course, two sides to this debate because some of our Dartmoor ghosts have been appearing and reappearing over a long period of time. At one haunted property a man said of the ghost there, 'I'm sure she has some unfinished business to complete...'

I remember too once taking Alan Nance to a haunted valley and as we were leaving he said, 'This is such a beautiful place I'm not surprised the spirits keep coming back.'

Perhaps this is why Dartmoor in general is such haunted territory. It could be that a combination of the varied beauty and its powerful, energising atmosphere get hold of people in such a way that they are reluctant to let go – even in death.

Some concluding thoughts on Dartmoor – and the supernatural

Ghosts frequently appear in a matter-of-fact way. Marlene Lethbridge, who was born at Chagford, had a typical experience. She told me: 'I had a curious sighting one day in the car with my husband Bob who was at the wheel. We were travelling back from a trip to Exeter. We were about 300 yards from the Fingle Bridge turning when suddenly a man in a grey cloak with a black dog started crossing the main road. The odd thing is they were walking above the level of the present road. Very odd but they were there all right. Bob saw them and swerved to avoid them.'

Some of us believe there is 'an invisible third ear' which picks up things below the surface of everyday life. A good deal has been happening – and continues to happen – below the surface of Dartmoor. In fact we are making great strides forward: we now have a vast accumulation of supernatural evidence, and more and more men and women are expressing an intelligent interest in the subject. When Colin Wilson began researching for a book entitled *Afterlife*, he was unsure about the evidence for life after death.

But by the time he came to write its postscript he said the evidence 'points unmistakably to survival'.

The media at long last are beginning to treat the supernatural with the respect it deserves. And parapsychology is now recognised by many as a genuine cause. An important sea change is taking place: in the last forty years the distinction between the natural and the supernatural has become less and less marked. Later in this century such distinction may become altogether meaningless.

I write these words on a day when Dartmoor looks glorious in that distant blue haze, and it reminds me, if ever I needed reminding, that baffling, fascinating events take place on and around the moor. They seem to confirm the fact that where ghosts appear they are likely to reappear.

I believe, before the twenty-first century grows old, there will be major breakthroughs in the supernatural field and, on past evidence, there's a strong chance of at least one of those breakthroughs happening on Dartmoor.

That is an exciting prospect.